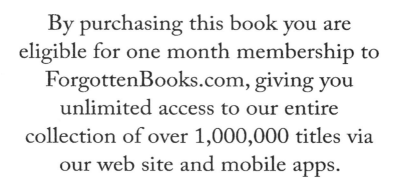

ISBN 978-0-331-17965-1
PIBN 11023420

Watkins Cook Book

A composite grouping of all the manufacturing and administrative properties of The J. R. Watkins Company. These many buildings house the model facilities so essential to creation of superior products for the home.

The J. R. Watkins Company

FROM OCEAN TO OCEAN

New York   Chicago   Boston   Newark   Columbus   Kansas City
Winona   Memphis   Oakland
Montreal   Hamilton   Winnipeg   Vancouver

CONTENTS

THE SECRET OF ARTISTIC, APPEALING MEALS

ONLY a woman appreciates the nagging worry of planning and preparing meals day after day. What countless millions have voiced this soul-wrung mealtime cry, "Oh, what shall I cook?" And don't you find that endless planning even worse than the work of preparing?

Woman certainly deserves better than to be sacrificed to that nightmarish horror of pots, pans and plans, which steals away the joy from the whole day, each mealtime.

How amazingly you enjoy the meal someone else had to do the worrying about and preparing. You can make each mealtime just such a pleasurable occasion for yourself.

And it will be so easy, too.

Simply call upon Watkins good old-fashioned helps to make each meal a splendidly different treat—even to the most jaded appetite. Sixty years ago Watkins set out to build a business which served the housewife as only a tried and true friend would.

This little unpretentious book is an example of our effort to be helpful to you. Anyone could print a number of recipes on paper and call it a cook book. YOU alone could prove if it were, really.

Watkins spent eighteen months of expert investigation and test, so that every recipe was sure to be a cure for worry and make the food of a novice rival that of the French chef.

And by using those superb Watkins "custom-made" quality spices, flavors and baking powder, you create your own insurance against failure.

Better still, each item of the meal, be it breakfast or banquet, takes on a new, delicate, yet striking piquancy that defies expression in words. You can't understand this almost "spiritual" difference and fineness and you'll never achieve it without the use of Watkins "custom-made" quality.

Just put the compound double-distilled wisdom and experience of this little classic of cookery shoulder to shoulder with the magic working quality of Watkins "custom-made" cooking helps and you will have waved that fairy wand that makes mealtime pleasure time, besides assuring you food artistry second to none.

If this were a personal letter to you it could not carry a greater or more personal interest in making your daily life easier, more pleasant. If we were "cross-the-fence" neighbors, our sympathetic eagerness to be helpful in every way could be no greater. As one of our patrons said long ago, "Watkins is really the 'Soul of Service.'" Wasn't that simply a splendidly appreciative understanding of what this Company is really setting as its goal?

We want to be your friend and want to win for this Company, its service and products, a "reserved seat" in that warm spot in your heart which you open only to old and proved friends.

We are trying so hard, all the time, to make you call "Watkins" your friend. You have sensed something wonderfully and old-fashionedly solid and friendly behind Watkins, haven't you? Now don't ever hesitate to write any suggestion or criticism which you feel would help us to still more help you and that great and wonderfully noble sisterhood—The Housewife.

Very true, this is a big, big business. A "Ten Million Dollar Corporation" it is called in the world of business and finance, and yet, back of those high sounding words, back behind the scenes, what do you find?

Just a few humans—a few men, a few women. Just people like yourself, their hearts beat, they breathe. Blood, not ice water, runs warm in their veins. Yes, there are just a few of us humans who are responsible to you—striving, and hoping every minute, to win your appreciation for the real common sense human interest and helpfulness we try to give you as a result of our effort.

Back of a desk maybe a thousand miles from you as you read this, we miss the ring of your voice, the cheer of your smile, and the stimulus of your friendly advice. The only measure we have of your friendliness is your liking for the products and helps our hand and brains devise for your pleasure, comfort, health. You and the tens of millions of yous affected by our service are sitting every minute of every day as judges. Most excellent, fair and critical judges of this marvelous and time-enduring service and quality everyone recognizes as—"Watkins."

For nearly a full three score years Watkins has met that test and trial. Without that "Soul of Service" we could never have survived that acid test of time. And so today, tomorrow, and every minute of every today and tomorrow to come, this Company has consecrated itself to human, personal interest in you—to do all humanly possible to give you more, better and for less, and this in competition with the whole world, and that is our Pledge to you—our "Soul of Service."

Every recipe in this booklet is a gem. Their results will surpass your fondest hopes. Are you longing for a delicate, delicious sponge cake that even the baby can eat safely? Long for it no more. Turn to page 36. There your wish is fulfilled. There is just one caution. Be sure to use Watkins Better Baking Powder and super-excellent Vanilla. Unless you do this, you will be unable to achieve that wondrous delicacy which caused this recipe to be adopted.

Possibly a rich, buttery conception—a French pastry is what you need for some really special occasion. Why worry or gamble? You will never find anything so richly delightful as Cocoa Marshmallow Roll on page 49. And so simple and so easy you can unfailingly produce just such toothsome wonders by always following Watkins recipes and using Watkins "custom-made" quality ingredients.

You and we are all one big family. Won't you please help us with your interest and friendly advice, either as to our products or service? Just write to the Public Relations Department, The J. R. Watkins Company, Winona, Minn.

SOUPS

CREAM OF TOMATO SOUP

2 tablespoons flour	1 teaspoon celery salt
1½ tablespoons butter	Salt, and Watkins Black
1 cup milk	Pepper to taste
2½ cups strained tomato juice	Pinch of baking soda

Blend butter and flour together in saucepan, add milk and bring to boiling point. Heat tomato juice and add soda and seasonings. Just before serving, add butter, flour and milk mixture to tomato juice and stir till boiling. Serve hot. A spoon of whipped cream may be used to top it, and buttered croutons are excellent to serve with it.

To make croutons, butter two slices of bread, cut in cubes, and toast in oven until a light brown and crisp.

POTATO SOUP

1 quart milk	4 potatoes
1 tablespoon butter	1 teaspoon salt
½ teaspoon celery salt	3 eggs

Boil and mash the potatoes; add the butter and salt and the celery salt; scald the milk and add to the potato mixture; beat the eggs well; stir quickly into soup and when boiling point is reached, serve immediately with 1 tablespoon of whipped cream in each dish.

OYSTER STEW

1 pint oysters	1 teaspoon salt
1 quart scalded milk	Dash of Watkins Black and
2 tablespoons butter	Red Pepper

Clean oysters and strain the liquor. Heat the liquor to boiling point, add oysters and cook until the edges curl, which will be only a few minutes. Combine liquor and scalded milk, add seasoning and butter and serve. Do not throw away the oyster liquor. Oysters do not require long cooking.

VEGETABLE SOUP

To 1 quart of stock or bouillon, add 3 tablespoons each of celery and turnip or potato, either chopped or cut with a vegetable cutter; 1 tablespoon carrot and 1 cup of cooked and strained tomato and a little fried onion; or omit the tomato and onion and add small green peas, cauliflower, asparagus tips, or all three. Any number of combinations may be made up including beans, rice, corn and other vegetables.

NOODLES FOR SOUP

2 eggs	Pinch of salt
2 tablespoons water	1 cup of flour

Beat, stir and knead in flour as much as possible. Roll out in thin sheets and let lay on cloth until nearly dry. Roll up and cut very fine. Have broth nicely seasoned and boiling. Drop in noodles and cook 15 to 20 minutes.

MEATS

JELLIED VEAL LOAF

Three pounds veal shoulder and knuckle joints, ½ pound of salt pork; boil together until it drops from bones. Chop cucumber pickles, parsley and green pepper, 4 hard-boiled eggs; add to chopped meat. Boil down liquor and put in enough to moisten the whole. Press in mould.

VEAL BIRDS

Cut thin slices of veal steak into 2½ by 3 inch pieces, or slightly larger; pound. Make a bread dressing, using nuts and raisins with the bread crumbs. Place small amount of dressing into each piece of veal; roll up and fasten with toothpicks. Brown birds in spider in 2 tablespoons hot butter and lard. Pour into baking dish, pour drippings from spider over. Make a cream gravy with 3 cups of milk, 1 large tablespoon butter, 1 tablespoon flour, salt and pepper. Pour over birds, and bake in hot oven ½ hour. May be baked with more butter and without cream gravy, or may use milk for basting and add flour after the birds are taken out. Pork tenderloin is good used the same way.

BAKED HAM

Soak ham overnight, then wash and scrape it. Put it into cold water; let it come to boiling point then simmer for 2 hours. Let the ham cool in the water; then remove and draw off the skin. Bake in moderate oven for 2 hours, baste it frequently, using 1 cup of peach juice (left over from canned or pickled peaches or other fruits), 2 spoonfuls at a time; then baste with melted butter. When done cover with a paste of Watkins Prepared Mustard, flour and brown sugar moistened with peach juice, and return to oven to brown.

HAMBURG ROAST EN SURPRISE

1½ pounds round steak put through meat chopper
1 teaspoon onion juice
1 teaspoon salt
⅓ cup soft bread crumbs
1 egg beaten light
1 tablespoon finely chopped parsley
¼ teaspoon paprika

Mix all thoroughly and shape into long loaf in baking tin. Take out some of the mixture in center and drop in 3 or 4 raw eggs; cover with meat and sprinkle the top with buttered cracker crumbs or strips of bacon and cracker crumbs. Let bake about ½ hour, basting 5 or 6 times with drippings or hot fat from salt pork or bacon. Before meat is set to cook, add a pint of potato balls that have been boiled about 15 minutes and dried on cloth; baste with meat. This is good without eggs.

CHICKEN PIE

1 cup flour	¼ teaspoon Watkins Black
½ cup milk	Pepper
2 level tablespoons lard	2 cups milk or stock
1½ teaspoons Watkins Bak-	Cooked chicken
Powder	1 heaping tablespoon butter
½ teaspoon salt	1 heaping tablespoon flour

Melt the butter in the same pan in which pie is to be made. Combine with the flour and add the milk or chicken stock; season. When cooked creamy, add the chicken. Mix the biscuit dough, roll out ½ inch thick; cut with small biscuit cutter and cover the top of the chicken. Bake 25 minutes in moderate oven.

VEAL AND HAM PIE

Cut into squares, 2 pounds of veal cutlets and arrange a layer of these in the bottom of a deep baking dish. Sprinkle with salt and pepper, and a few slices of hard-cooked egg. Over these place a thin layer of fine chopped, cold, cooked ham. Make another

layer of veal, seasonings, egg and ham and so on until the dish is filled. Mushrooms, oysters and pieces of sweetbread are very nice additions to the pie. The pie is covered with a rich pastry. Bake for an hour to an hour and a half. Shortly before removing from oven, pour in through a hole in the crust, a cup of rich, brown gravy or stock. This may be eaten warm or cold.

CHICKEN A LA KING

Take white meat of boiled chicken; cut into dice and put into saucepan on stove. Moisten with hot cream to cover chicken; add 1 sweet red pepper cut into small pieces, salt and pepper. Let simmer gently for 15 minutes and then remove to side of stove. Beat yolk of an egg; mix with cream and chicken, but do not allow to boil. Add piece of butter size of walnut; serve at once, very hot on toast.

JIGGS' FAVORITE

4 pounds corned beef	2 small turnips
4 beets	6 potatoes
1 small cabbage	3 onions
4 carrots	6 parsnips

Wash the meat and let stand in water ½ hour to remove some of the salt. Put in a kettle with boiling water to cover and simmer about 4 hours. Prepare the vegetables and cut the cabbage into quarters. Remove the meat when tender. Add the carrots, turnips and cabbage and cook 2 hours and add the potatoes the last half hour. Add the cooked beets and the meat. Heat all together and serve on a large platter with the vegetables around the meat.

BEEF LOAF

2 pounds lean beef	2 tablespoons melted butter
1 large piece of bread	Dash of Watkins Pepper
2 eggs	2 cups sweet milk
	Salt

Put the beef through food chopper; add the bread crumbs and well-beaten eggs; then the melted butter and seasoning; add enough sweet milk to form into a loaf; put into deep baking pan and bake in a moderate oven until when pierced with fork the juice will not be red. Turn on a platter and serve hot or cold.

FISH

SALMON LOAF

1 can salmon	1 cup stale bread crumbs
2 eggs	½ cup milk
1 teaspoon lemon juice	1 teaspoon salt

Mince the salmon and remove the bones. Add the bread crumbs, beaten eggs and the milk. Season with salt and lemon juice. Put into well greased molds and steam or bake 30 minutes. Turn from the mold, serve hot or cold with white sauce, sour sauce or lemon.

BAKED FISH

Clean fish carefully, wipe and dry. Rub fish well with salt, stuff with dressing made of 1 cup stale bread crumbs, ½ teaspoon salt, 1 tablespoon minced parsley, 1 tablespoon melted butter. Dash of Watkins Pepper, few drops of onion juice and lukewarm water enough to moisten. Lay strips of bacon over top of fish to provide necessary fat, and baste often with melted butter and water. When done, remove to platter carefully and serve with butter sauce, garnish with parsley and lemon.

TROUT

Clean fish and dry between towels. Sprinkle with salt and pepper, dip into flour, crumbs or corn meal, then egg and again into crumbs. Fry in deep fat. Drain on paper and garnish with lemon and parsley.

PIGS IN BLANKET

Dry large oysters. Pin around each thin slices of bacon and fasten with toothpicks. Fry or brown in very hot oven; serve with lemon.

CODFISH BALLS

Boil codfish thoroughly; boil potatoes and mash together; add 1 egg, butter, cream, salt and pepper; fry in hot fat.

SALMON CROQUETTES

1 can salmon	3 well beaten eggs
1 large cup rolled cracker or	Butter size of an egg
bread crumbs	Pinch of salt and Watkins Pepper

Moisten with cream until proper consistency to mould into oblong shapes. Dip each croquette in beaten egg and cracker dust and cook in deep fat.

CREAMED TUNA FISH ON TOAST

Melt 2 tablespoons butter and blend with it 3 tablespoons flour; add 2 cups of milk, and stir while cooking until the mixture is smooth and thick. Add 1 teaspoon salt, 1/4 teaspoon Watkins Black and Red Pepper, 1 small can of pimentos chopped. Cook 3 minutes, stirring constantly and add 1 cup flaked tuna fish (canned). Serve hot on squares of toast.

CLAM CHOWDER

1 quart clams	1 tablespoon salt
4 cups potatoes cut in dice	4 tablespoons butter
1½ inch cube fat salt pork	1 quart scalded milk
1 onion diced	8 unsalted soda crackers

Remove dark part from soft part of clams and chop hard parts finely. Reserve clam water, heat and strain it. Cut pork in small pieces, fry out and strain into stewpan. Parboil potatoes 5 minutes, drain and put a layer in bottom of stewpan; add chopped clams, sprinkle with salt and pepper and dredge with flour; add remaining potatoes, sprinkle with salt and pepper and dredge with flour. Add 2½ cups boiling water; cook 10 minutes; add milk, soft part of clams and butter. Boil 3 minutes and add crackers split in halves. Reheat clam water, thicken with 1 tablespoon flour and 1 of butter and add with the remainder of the butter just before serving. The crackers may be omitted and used in the bottom of the serving plates, when the chowder is served.

CHEESE AND EGG DISHES

CHEESE TOAST

4 slices bread	¼ cup grated cheese
½ cup milk	Salt and Watkins Red Pepper to taste

Remove crusts from bread and fry a delicate brown in hot fat. Remove from fat and place in warm milk until moist. Cover with grated cheese. Sprinkle on the salt and red pepper and bake 5 minutes in a hot oven. Serve at once.

SCALLOPED CHEESE BREAD

4 slices buttered bread	2 cups milk
¾ cup grated cheese	¼ teaspoon salt
2 beaten eggs	Few grains Watkins Red Pepper

Line a buttered pudding dish with the slices of bread and cover these with the grated cheese and a few grains of Watkins Red Pepper. Beat the eggs slightly, add the salt and milk. Pour this mixture over the bread and cheese and bake 15 minutes in a hot oven.

CHEESE STRAWS

1 cup grated cheese	2 slices of bread without crust
1 tablespoon butter creamed	4 tablespoons cold water

Dry the bread in the oven and roll into crumbs. Combine with the cheese, butter, water, and add salt, Watkins Red Pepper and flour enough to roll out. Cut in strips and bake delicate brown.

CHEESE FONDUE

1 tablespoon butter	2 cups grated cheese
1 cup fresh milk	2 eggs
1 cup fine bread crumbs	1 saltspoon Watkins Mustard

Melt butter, add 2 tablespoons flour, then milk gradually. Stir until they boil, cool a little, add cheese and yolks and seasonings. Fold in whites stiffly beaten. Pour into buttered baking dish. Bake 20 minutes in hot oven. Serve hot.

WELSH RAREBIT

Bread toasted on one side
½ pound soft mild cheese
1 tablespoon butter
¼ teaspoon salt

¼ teaspoon Watkins Mustard
Few grains Watkins Red Pepper
⅓ cup milk or cream
1 egg

Cut the cheese in small pieces. Melt the butter, then add the cheese and seasoning; as the cheese melts, add milk gradually, while stirring constantly; then egg, slightly beaten. Serve on the untoasted side of the bread. The rarebit should be smooth and creamy and not stringy.

BREAD AND CHEESE OMELET

½ cup bread crumbs
½ cup milk
4 eggs
¾ teaspoon salt

⅛ teaspoon Watkins Black
Pepper
1 tablespoon butter
3 tablespoons grated cheese

Soak crumbs 15 minutes in milk, add the salt, pepper, well-beaten eggs and grated cheese. Have a frying pan heated, and melt 1 tablespoon of butter in it. Into this pour the egg mixture and place on range where it will cook evenly. When deliciously browned underneath, place pan in oven to finish cooking on top. Remove from oven, fold and turn on a hot platter; this makes an excellent luncheon dish. Serve with currant jelly.

CHEESE BALLS

Whites of 3 eggs beaten with ½ cup grated cheese. To each egg add a pinch of salt, cayenne pepper. Form into balls; roll each ball in cracker crumbs. Fry in hot lard like croquettes.

ENGLISH MONKEY

1 cup bread crumbs
Hot buttered toast
1 cup milk
1 egg

1 tablespoon butter
¾ cup grated cheese
½ teaspoon salt
Few grains Watkins Red Pepper

Soak the bread crumbs 15 minutes in milk. Melt the butter and add the cheese. When cheese has melted, add the soaked crumbs and seasoning. Mix well together and add the beaten egg. Cook 3 minutes and pour over hot buttered toast. Serve at once.

VEGETABLES

STUFFED PEPPERS

Pour boiling water over peppers; let stand 1 minute. Chop fine 1 slice of cold ham. Melt 1 tablespoon butter; add 1 minced onion and fry until brown. Add ham, 3 slices tomato. Cook 10 minutes and add fine bread crumbs until quite thick. Fill pepper cases and bake 1 hour in tomato juice.

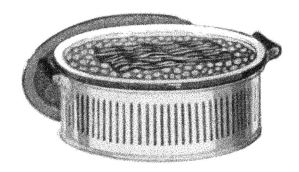

WATKINS BAKED BEANS

1 quart navy beans	1 tablespoon brown sugar
½ pound sliced bacon	1 teaspoon Watkins Ginger
1 teaspoon soda	2 tablespoons molasses
1 teaspoon Watkins ground Mustard	1 tablespoon salt

Pick over and soak the beans over night. In the morning scald in hot soda water; drain; then add fresh water to cover and cook 15 minutes or until you can blow skins off when trying. Pour off all the water; put beans in a stone baking jar; add the other ingredients; cover with fresh water and bake 4 or 5 hours with the cover on the jar. Remove the cover the last half hour.

STUFFED BAKED POTATOES

Bake potatoes, scoop out, season and add cream, butter, salt and Watkins Black Pepper. Beat very light; refill shells and sprinkle with cracker crumbs and butter, grated cheese, or bits of bacon cut fine. Brown in oven.

SUCCOTASH

1 dozen ears sweet corn	1 quart lima beans
1 cup meat stock, gravy or water	1 cup milk
	Watkins Black Pepper
1 tablespoon butter	1 teaspoon salt

Cut the corn from the cob; add the lima beans, meat stock or water and let simmer slowly until the liquid is absorbed and the corn and beans are tender; then add the seasoning, milk and butter; cook for 10 minutes and serve in a covered dish.

STUFFED ONIONS

6 medium sized onions	Salt and Watkins Pepper
6 tablespoons bread crumbs	Boiling water to moisten
½ cup nut meats	

Remove outer skins of onions and parboil 10 minutes. Remove inside with fork or spoon. Chop fine; put in saucepan and mix with crumbs, nuts and seasoning and 1 tablespoon butter. Moisten with boiling water and cook 5 minutes. Have a creamy substance rather than wet. Refill shells, sprinkle with buttered crumbs over top and brown in oven.

BAKED SQUASH

Pare, and remove seeds of 2 medium sized squashes; cut into thin slices. Brush a casserole with bacon drippings or butter, and put into it the squash, a little salt, pepper and half a cup of water. Bake in a slow oven until tender. Before serving mix with a fork or an egg whip.

Squash may be baked in the shell, placing the shell in a shallow pan of water, and baking until tender. Remove the outer skin, and season squash with butter, salt and pepper to taste.

Page Seventeen

PEAS AND POTATOES

Mash potatoes, add butter and salt; make in thick cakes; fry in hot lard. Fill each with green peas and put cover on. Serve hot with baked ham.

STRING BEANS

If fresh beans are used, pick them over and remove ends and strings. Boil for ½ hour or until tender; then drain them and add 1 tablespoon butter, 2 tablespoons cream, season to taste and serve after 10 minutes slow cooking on the back of the stove. If canned beans are used, it is not necessary to cook until tender, simply heat them well, drain and add butter and cream as above.

CABBAGE AU GRATIN

Boil small, hard head cabbage cut in pieces in salted water, uncovered for 30 minutes. Drain in colander. Butter baking dish and arrange a layer of cabbage in it, cover with white sauce and then another layer of cabbage until dish is filled. Cover top with buttered crumbs; add a small quantity of milk and bake 15 minutes to brown.

FRIED BEETS

Boil 8 medium sized beets until tender in salted water. Drain, remove outer skins and cut in slices. Have a generous amount of butter hot in frying pan, add beets, season with salt and Watkins Black Pepper and fry until crisp and thoroughly heated in butter. These must be watched, as they are very apt to burn on short notice.

MACARONI WITH SPINACH

Cook 2 pounds of spinach in the water that clings to the leaves, after thoroughly washing it. Press through a colander when cooked. Have ready, ½ pound of cooked macaroni and 2 cups of grated cheese. Proceed to arrange these in layers in the order given in a buttered baking dish, until dish is filled. Cover with buttered crumbs and bake in oven. Garnish with slices of hard-cooked egg and sliced tomato when serving.

EGG PLANT

Cut in thick slices and salt well, allowing to stand for some time. Drain off water that gathers, dip in beaten egg to which 1 tablespoon of cold water has been added, then in bread crumbs and fry on hot griddle with plenty of hot fat.

CARROTS SUPREME

Wash and scrape 2 pounds of carrots, and slice. Add to ½ cup of melted butter in a saucepan. Season with 1 tablespoon chopped parsley, ½ tablespoon minced onion, dash of Watkins Nutmeg, and toss the whole over the fire until the carrots are all coated with butter and thoroughly hot. Add 2 cups of meat stock, cover and let the whole simmer for 20 to 30 minutes, then add 2 tablespoons flour made into a paste with cold water, and blended smooth with a little of the stock from the saucepan. Stir until this boils up through carrots and serve the whole in deep vegetable dish, garnished with small sausages.

CREAMED KOHL RABI

Peel and slice kohl rabi and boil 20 minutes in salted water, or until nearly tender. Arrange in a baking dish in layers with white sauce. Season each layer with pepper and salt, sprinkle the top with bread crumbs and bake 20 minutes.

GLAZED SWEET POTATOES

Boil sweet potatoes until tender. Drain and peel and cut in slices. Arrange in shallow buttered baking dish in layers, covering each layer with butter and sprinkling generously with brown sugar. Add a small quantity of water and bake in oven 15 to 20 minutes.

FRENCH FRIED POTATOES

Wash and pare small potatoes, cut in eighths lengthwise and soak 1 hour in cold salted water. Take from water, dry between towels, and fry in deep fat. Drain on brown paper.

BREAD AND ROLLS

BREAD—Slow Process

¾ dry yeast cake	4 tablespoons salt
3 pints water	3 tablespoons lard
8 tablespoons sugar	Flour

Break up yeast into 1 cup lukewarm water. Beat in enough flour to make a stiff batter. Cover and let stand in warm place for an hour. Add sugar, salt and lard to 5 cups lukewarm water. Beat in enough flour to make a stiff batter. Add yeast and enough flour to knead. Knead until light and elastic. Put in covered pan. Let rise 10 hours in a temperature of not less than 65° F. In the morning, shape into loaves, put into greased tins, having tins one-half full. Let rise to double its bulk. Bake from 45 minutes to an hour in a moderate oven. This recipe will make 4 loaves.

BREAD—Quick Process

1 compressed yeast cake	4 tablespoons salt
3 pints water	3 tablespoons lard
8 tablespoons sugar	Flour

Dissolve yeast in cup lukewarm water, make a sponge of 5 cups lukewarm water and dissolved yeast with enough flour to make a stiff batter. Beat well. Cover and stand in a warm place for 2 hours or until light and full of bubbles. Add sugar, salt and lard. Mix in enough flour to knead stiff. Let raise for 2 hours or until double its bulk. Shape into loaves and put into greased bread tins. Let rise again for about 45 minutes. Bake from 45 minutes to an hour in a moderate oven. This recipe makes 4 loaves.

BRAN BREAD

2 cups boiling water or half milk	1½ cups white flour
2 tablespoons shortening	3½ cups bran
¼ cup sugar	¼ cup lukewarm water
	1 cake compressed yeast

Put salt, shortening and sugar in a bowl and pour on the hot liquid. Cool and when lukewarm add the yeast dissolved in the warm water, then the flour. Beat hard, let rise to double its bulk and beat again vigorously. Half fill well greased bread tins with the mixture and let double its bulk again. Bake in a hot oven 45 to 50 minutes, or bake in individual gem pans 25 to 30 minutes.

PARKER HOUSE ROLLS

3 cups scalded milk	3 tablespoons sugar
1 cake compressed yeast dissolved in lukewarm water	4 tablespoons shortening (½ butter and ½ lard) Pinch of salt

Let your milk cool until it is lukewarm, add shortening, sugar, salt and dissolved yeast. Beat in 4 cups of flour and cover. Let rise where it is warm. When light, add enough flour to knead (about 5 cups). Let rise until double in bulk, then roll out with rolling pin to ¼ inch thickness. Cut with cookie cutter, brush with butter, fold over and press edges together. Let rise until very light. Bake 15 minutes in hot oven.

To make cinnamon rolls, make as for Parker House Rolls, when rolled out, brush with melted butter, sprinkle with sugar and Watkins Cinnamon. Roll up the dough and cut off rolls an inch thick. Place in buttered pan, let rise and bake.

THREE DAY BISCUITS

1 cake yeast	1 cup lukewarm water

Put above ingredients together and let stand until evening. Then stir in flour enough to make a thick batter and let stand over night. In the morning add 2 cups lukewarm water, ¾ cup sugar, generous ½ cup lard, 1 teaspoon salt. Stiffen with flour and knead until nice and smooth. Let it rise and knead it down three or four times during the day. If you wish to have fresh biscuits for breakfast the next day, put the biscuits in a pan at night and let rise until morning, when they are ready to put in the oven. The remaining dough may be kept in the ice box to use as you desire. These are delicious.

HOT BREADS

BAKING POWDER BISCUITS

2 cups flour	4 tablespoons shortening
1 teaspoon salt	¾ cup liquid (water or milk)

4 teaspoons Watkins Baking Powder

Sift the dry ingredients, cut in the shortening, then the liquid and knead slightly. Toss on a floured board, pat, roll lightly ¾ inch thick and cut. Place in an ungreased pan and bake in a hot oven about 12 minutes.

COCOA BISCUITS

2 cups flour	4 tablespoons shortening
1 teaspoon salt	¾ cup liquid
4 teaspoons Watkins Baking Powder.	2 tablespoons Watkins Cocoa

Sift the dry ingredients, cut in the shortening, then the liquid and knead slightly. Toss on a floured board, pat, roll lightly ¾ inch thick and cut. Place in an ungreased pan and bake in a hot oven about 12 minutes.

Bre
thei
Dro
min

WATKINS GINGERBREAD

4 level tablespoons sugar
4 level tablespoons butter
½ level teaspoon soda
1 level teaspoon Watkins Ginger
1 level teaspoon Watkins Cinnamon

1 egg
4 tablespoons molasses
4 tablespoons milk
1 level teaspoon Watkins Baking Powder
1 level cup flour

Break the egg into a bowl and beat for 2 minutes with an egg beater; then add the materials in the order named and beat thoroughly. Drop into well greased gem pans or into cake pans. Bake 15 minutes in moderate oven.

WATKINS TEA BISCUITS

1 cup sugar
½ cup butter
1 egg

2 teaspoons Watkins Baking
  Powder
½ cup milk
2 cups flour

Beat the butter and sugar to a cream, add the well beaten egg, salt and milk, and sift in the flour and baking powder together. It should make a very light dough, but if too soft, a little more flour may be added. Roll out on a well floured board and cut out with a biscuit cutter. Place close together in a shallow biscuit pan. Bake about 10 minutes and serve hot.

NUT BREAD

2 cups flour
½ cup chopped English
  walnuts
2 heaping tablespoons sugar

1 tablespoon melted butter
2 teaspoons Watkins Baking
  Powder
1½ cups sweet milk
Pinch of salt

Mix well together; put in bread tin; let stand one hour and bake one hour in slow oven.

WATKINS MUFFINS

3 cups flour	4 level teaspoons Watkins
1 teaspoon salt	Baking Powder
4 tablespoons melted butter	2 tablespoons sugar
1 egg	1½ cups milk

Sift dry materials; add the milk into which the egg beaten slightly is added, then the melted shortening. Mix thoroughly and quickly, cutting the dough back and forth. Drop into deep gem pans. Brush top with melted butter and bake 25 minutes. This recipe makes one dozen muffins. One pan of 6 muffins may be placed in the refrigerator to be baked and served hot for a ylater meal.

POPOVERS

2 cups flour	2 cups milk
1 teaspoon salt	3 eggs

Beat eggs for 5 minutes, add milk, then graduall stir in flour and salt, which have been previously sifted. Beaty with egg beater until full of air bubbles. Fill hot greased gem pans two-thirds full of the mixture, then bake in hot oven until brown, 30 or 40 minutes. This makes one dozen.

NUT AND RAISIN LOAF

3 cups flour
½ cup sugar
3 teaspoons Watkins Baking Powder

2 cups chopped English walnuts or 1 cup nuts and 1 cup raisins

Use 1 cup sweet milk or enough water to make a stiff batter. Let rise 20 minutes. Bake in slow oven for 45 minutes. This is very nice for sandwiches.

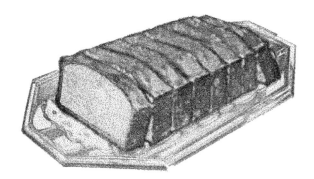

WATKINS CORN BREAD

1 cup yellow corn meal
¾ cup milk
2 tablespoons melted shortening
½ teaspoon salt

½ cup white flour
1 egg
1 tablespoon sugar
1½ teaspoons Watkins Baking Powder

Sift the dry ingredients together, whip up the egg in a measuring cup. Stir in the milk and pour into the other ingredients. Add the melted shortening, and mix thoroughly by cutting batter back and forth. Pour into baking pan, brush top with melted butter and bake in moderate oven 25 minutes. This recipe makes 6 large corn muffins or corn bread for 4 people.

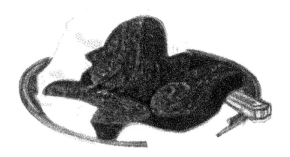

WATKINS STEAMED BROWN BREAD

½ cup graham flour   ½ teaspoon soda dissolved
½ cup yellow corn meal   in milk
½ cup flour   ¼ cup milk
½ teaspoon salt   ¾ cup dark molasses

1 egg beaten very light and added last

This batter is rather thin. Use empty Watkins Baking Powder tins, well greased and steam 3 or 4 hours. Bake in oven 5 minutes. Seeded raisins are very nice in this.

MARY'S RAISING BISCUITS

Boil 3 potatoes, mash, beat light. Rub butter size of walnut, and lard size of hen's egg into 2 quarts of flour. Add salt, a scant tablespoon of sugar, then potato and white of 1 egg beaten light and ½ compressed yeast cake dissolved in warm water; add enough warm water to make mixing dough. Let rise, put biscuits in pan, let rise again and bake.

GRIDDLE CAKES AND WAFFLES

SWEET MILK GRIDDLE CAKES

2 cups flour	1 egg
4 teaspoons Watkins Baking Powder	2 cups milk
½ teaspoon salt	2 tablespoons melted butter
	2 tablespoons sugar

Mix and sift dry ingredients. Add milk and well beaten egg slowly. Beat hard and add melted butter. Heat a griddle, and grease with a piece of fat salt pork or drippings. Aluminum griddles do not require greasing. Pour batter on griddle. When puffed up and full of bubbles, turn and cook other side. Serve at once.

CORN MEAL CAKES

1 cup milk	1 cup flour
1 egg	2 teaspoons Watkins Baking Powder
¾ cup corn meal	
¼ teaspoon salt	

Add beaten egg to milk, and add to dry ingredients which have been well mixed. Fry on hot griddle and serve at once.

BREAD CRUMB GRIDDLE CAKES

2 tablespoons butter	½ cup flour
2¼ cups scalded milk	3 teaspoons Watkins Baking Powder
1½ cups dry bread crumbs	
1 egg well beaten	½ teaspoon salt

Add butter to scalded milk and pour over bread crumbs. Let stand 10 minutes or until crumbs are soft. Add beaten egg and combine with flour, baking powder and salt. If crumbs are not dry, it is not necessary to use as much liquid.

POTATO PANCAKES OR OMELET

To 1 medium sized grated raw potato add 1 egg, 2 tablespoons milk, 1 tablespoon flour, salt and a little minced onion (if desired) or parsley. If too thin add a little more flour. Bake as for omelet or pancakes.

WAFFLES

2 eggs	1½ teaspoons salt
1½ cups sweet milk	4 teaspoons Watkins Baking
2 cups flour	Powder
1 tablespoon sugar	4 teaspoons melted shortening

Beat eggs until very light, and add milk. Sift and mix dry ingredients and add to eggs and milk. Add shortening and beat well. The batter should be thin enough to pour well, and should be smooth and full of bubbles. In place of the sweet milk and baking powder, sour milk may be used in the same proportion, using 1 teaspoon of soda to a cup of milk.

Cook in a hot waffle iron, well greased if of iron. Aluminum waffle molds need no greasing. Serve with maple syrup, or strained honey.

FRITTERS

FRITTER BATTER

2 eggs	2 tablespoons melted butter
1 cup flour	½ cup cold water
1 teaspoon salt	1 teaspoon sugar (if for fruit fritters)

Stir salt in egg yolk, add butter slowly, then sugar and when well mixed, stir in the flour slowly. Then add the water a little at a

time. Beat well, set aside for 2 hours, then stir in beaten whites of eggs. Batter must be thick. If not soft enough, add white of another egg, or small quantity of milk.

Roll fruit in powdered sugar, dip into the batter before the sugar has time to dissolve and drop quickly into hot fat and fry like doughnuts; drain on plain paper, roll in powdered sugar just before serving and serve hot. Oranges, bananas, prunes, apples or oysters may be used with this batter.

SOUTHERN APPLE FRITTERS

1 cup milk	4 chopped apples
2 eggs	¼ teaspoon salt
2 tablespoons sugar	Dash of Watkins Cinnamon
2 tablespoons melted butter	2 cups flour
2 teaspoons Watkins Baking Powder	

Beat the eggs into milk, add sugar, butter, salt and cinnamon. Mix thoroughly, then stir in flour and baking powder which have been sifted. Stir in the apples chopped fine. Fry in deep fat and sprinkle with powdered sugar.

PINEAPPLE FRITTERS

1 cup flour	¼ teaspoon salt
¾ cup milk	1 tablespoon melted butter
2 eggs	1 tablespoon sugar
2 teaspoons Watkins Baking Powder	8 thin slices pineapple

Sift dry ingredients into a bowl, beat the eggs, add milk to dry ingredients, then the beaten eggs and melted butter. Dip fruit in batter and fry in deep fat. Serve with lemon sauce.

LEMON SAUCE

1 tablespoon cornstarch	2 cups boiling water
1 cup sugar	2 tablespoons butter
Juice of 1 lemon and a bit of grated rind	

Mix cornstarch and sugar, add water and cook for 20 minutes. Add grated rind and juice of lemon and butter and serve very hot.

RICE AND CHERRY FRITTERS

1½ cups steamed rice	⅔ cup fresh sweetened cherries
2 tablespoons butter	or preserved cherries drained

1 well beaten egg

Mix ingredients in order given. Pour into a shallow pan; let stand until cool. Cut in squares, dip in crumbs, egg and crumbs again. Fry in deep fat. Roll in powdered sugar and serve with cherry sauce made by thickening cherry juice with cornstarch and adding juice of 1 lemon.

CORN FRITTERS

1 can corn	1 saltspoon salt
1 teaspoon Watkins Baking	2 eggs
Powder	½ cup flour

Add dry ingredients mixed and sifted well to corn. Then add beaten yolks of eggs and fold in beaten whites. Drop the mixture by tablespoonfuls into deep fat and brown.

CAKES AND COOKIES

MARBLE COCOA CAKE

2 cups flour sifted 3 times	3 egg whites
1 cup sugar	⅔ cup sweet milk
½ cup butter	½ teaspoon Watkins Vanilla

3 teaspoons Watkins Baking Powder

Cream butter and sugar. Sift flour and add baking powder, then sift again. Add milk and flour alternately to creamed mixture, add flavoring and the beaten whites of eggs. Separate the batter and to one-half add 3 teaspoons Watkins Cocoa, ½ teaspoon each of Watkins Nutmeg, Cinnamon and Allspice and ¼ teaspoon soda. Beat well and drop into a pan with horn in middle, first white then dark batter. Bake 45 minutes in moderate oven. Ice with confectioner's icing made by beating 1½ cups confectioner's sugar and 3 tablespoons cream and ½ teaspoon Watkins Lemon or Pineapple Extract.

Food that Tastes Good because it is delicious when pre[par]ed [with] Watkins Spices [and] Extracts

IN HAPPY HOMES you will find good foods finely flavored with Watkins Pure Spices and Extracts.

When Nature produces finer raw materials [we will use them.]
Meanwhile Watkins Quality c[ontinues supreme.]

ause **it is Good becomes supremely**
hen **prepared with**
s **Spices and**
Extracts

THE GOOD COOK
cooks better, with
far greater economy
when Watkins Qual-
ity Products are used.

materials Watkins will make better products.
s Quality continues supreme.

BROWN STONE FRONT CAKE

½ cup butter	½ cup hot water
1½ cups sugar	2 eggs
¾ cup Watkins Cocoa	1 teaspoon Watkins Vanilla
½ cup sweet milk	1 teaspoon soda

2 cups flour

Cream butter and sugar. Dissolve cocoa in hot water and add the eggs beaten. Add milk and flavoring. Dissolve soda in hot water and add flour. This makes a splendid cake and is a rich mahogany color.

FRUIT CAKE

2 cups brown sugar	2 teaspoons Watkins Cinnamon
⅔ cup shortening	1 teaspoon Watkins Cloves
2 cups water	1 teaspoon Watkins Nutmeg
2 cups raisins	½ teaspoon Watkins Allspice
2 cups currants	1 teaspoon salt

Stir this mixture together and cook for 3 minutes. Cool and add 4 cups flour, 2 small teaspoons soda, 2 teaspoons Watkins Baking Powder, and 1½ cups nut meats. Bake in 2 well greased loaf tins 45 minutes in moderate oven. Will keep indefinitely.

COCOANUT CAKE

1 cup sugar	½ cup butter
3 cups flour	1 cup milk
½ teaspoon salt	2 teaspoons Watkins Vanilla
4 eggs	3 teaspoons Watkins Baking Powder

Cream butter and sugar together, sift the flour, baking powder and salt and add alternately with the beaten yolks of eggs and milk. Beat thoroughly, then add stiffly beaten whites of eggs and flavoring and mix gently. Grease 3 layer tins, dust with flour and divide mixture. Bake in moderate oven 20 minutes. Use the following filling between layers and on top of cake:

FILLING FOR COCOANUT CAKE

1 teaspoon butter	1 teaspoon Watkins Vanilla
1 cup sugar	White of 1 egg
1 cup water	½ cup shredded cocoanut
Pinch of cream of tartar	¼ teaspoon salt

Boil water and sugar together, add butter and cream of tartar and boil until it forms soft ball in cold water. Beat white of egg to stiff froth, add salt, then pour in syrup gradually, add vanilla and beat until thick and cold. Spread on cake and sprinkle over with cocoanut. Enough for 3 layers.

CARAMEL SPONGE CAKE

1½ cups sugar
1¾ cup sifted pastry flour
3 level teaspoons Watkins
   Baking Powder

1 teaspoon Watkins Vanilla
4 eggs
½ cup boiling water
¼ teaspoon salt

Put 1 cup of the sugar in a pan and place the pan on the stove. Heat, stirring meanwhile, until the sugar is all melted and of a light brown color, but do not let it burn. Add the boiling water and stir until all lumps are dissolved. This makes about 1 cup of syrup. Beat the 4 egg whites until stiff. Add beaten yolks and the remaining half cup of sugar. Mix salt, baking powder and flour and add to the egg mixture alternately with the hot syrup. Add vanilla. Bake like any sponge cake in a moderate oven and frost with caramel frosting.

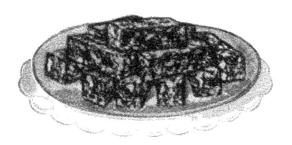

BROWNIES

1 cup brown sugar
1 egg
¼ cup melted butter

1 teaspoon Watkins Vanilla
1 cup chopped nuts
½ cup flour

2 tablespoons Watkins Cocoa

Mix and spread with knife in small pan. Bake in very moderate oven 20 minutes. Turn out of pan as soon as taken from oven and cut in strips about 1 x 4 inches. Roll in powdered sugar.

COCOA CREAM CAKE

¾ cup butter
2½ cups flour
2 tablespoons Watkins Cocoa
1 cup milk
3 eggs
1 cup sugar
3½ teaspoons Watkins Baking Powder
1 teaspoon Watkins Vanilla

Cream butter, blend in sugar and cocoa. Stir in the eggs one by one without previous beating. Sift baking powder with the flour and add alternately with milk to other mixture; then add extract. Bake in 2 or 3 layers and put together with the following frosting:

White of 1 egg
¾ cup confectioner's sugar
2 teaspoons cold water
½ teaspoon Watkins Vanilla

Beat white of egg until stiff; add water and sugar. Beat thoroughly, then add flavoring. Spread between layers and on top of cake.

CHOCOLATE CAKE

½ cup Watkins Cocoa
½ cup white sugar
½ cup sweet milk
Yolk of 1 egg

Boil well together and let cool

1 cup sugar
½ cup butter
2 eggs
½ cup sour milk into which 1 teaspoon soda has been dissolved. Mix both parts together and add 2 cups flour. Bake in moderate oven in layers. Ice with chocolate icing and nuts.

COCOA CAKE WITHOUT EGGS

2 cups brown sugar   1 cup sour milk or buttermilk
½ cup Watkins Cocoa   2½ cups flour
½ cup lard

Last of all add ½ cup hot water to which 1 level teaspoon soda has been added. This makes 3 big layers and is improved by adding 1 teaspoon Watkins Vanilla.

JELLY ROLL

4 eggs
1 cup sugar
2 tablespoons melted butter
2 cups flour
1 teaspoon Watkins Lemon Extract

1 teaspoon Watkins Baking Powder
¼ teaspoon salt
4 tablespoons milk
Jelly or preserves

Beat eggs and sugar together 20 minutes. Remove beater, sift in flour, salt and baking powder, add milk, extract and melted butter. Grease large flat tin, dust over with flour, pour in mixture and spread out evenly. Bake 12 minutes in moderate oven. Turn out on sugared paper, spread quickly with jelly or preserves and roll up at once. This cake will crack if spreading and rolling are not quickly done. Sliced jelly roll is delicious with custard.

PRINCE OF WALES CAKE

2 cups brown sugar	1 teaspoon Watkins Cinnamon
1 cup butter	1 teaspoon Watkins Nutmeg
1 cup sour milk	1 teaspoon Watkins Cloves
4 cups flour	2 tablespoons molasses
2 teaspoons soda	½ teaspoon Watkins Baking
2 egg yolks or 4 whole eggs	Powder

1 cup nuts and raisins mixed

Bake in loaf and frost with caramel frosting.

CREAM PUFFS

1 cup milk	4 eggs
1 cup flour sifted four times	Pinch of salt

1 tablespoon butter

Put milk in double boiler with butter; let boil, and add flour; let cook 2 minutes. Remove from fire; break in eggs, one at a time and beat well. Drop on pans; bake 20 minutes until crisp. Fill with custard or whipped cream when cool. Serve with hot chocolate or maple sauce, or sprinkle with powdered sugar.

COCOA COOKIES

½ cup shortening	½ cup Watkins Cocoa
1 cup sugar	4 teaspoons Watkins Baking
2 eggs	Powder
⅓ cup milk	4 cups flour

Cream the sugar and the shortening together; add the milk slowly, then the eggs well beaten and the cocoa; sift the flour and baking powder together and add to make a stiff dough. Roll out ¼ inch thick and cut. Bake in a hot oven 12 to 15 minutes. Decorate with white icing.

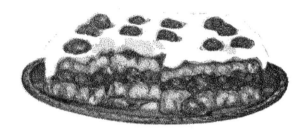

STRAWBERRY SHORTCAKE

2½ cups flour	Butter
5 teaspoons Watkins Baking	Strawberries
Powder	1½ cups sugar
½ teaspoon salt	Whipped cream
⅓ cup shortening	Sugar

Scant cup of milk

Sift together flour, baking powder and salt; work in shortening and then use milk as needed to mix to a soft dough. Spread the dough in two well greased pans and bake about 15 minutes. Turn one cake on a large plate, spread with butter, cover with straw-berries mixed with sugar; set the second cake above the berries, spread with butter and cover with the rest of the berries. Serve with or without cream.

DOUGHNUTS

2¾ cups sifted flour	½ tablespoon shortening
2 teaspoons Watkins Baking Powder	1 egg
	⅔ cup sugar
½ teaspoon salt	½ cup milk
½ teaspoon Watkins Nutmeg	

Sift together flour, baking powder, salt and nutmeg and work in shortening. Beat the egg, beat in sugar and milk and stir into the dry ingredients. Take out a little at a time on a floured board, roll into a sheet, cut out with a doughnut cutter and fry in deep fat. The fat is at the right heat when it browns a crumb of bread in 60 seconds.

FROSTINGS AND FILLINGS

BOILED FROSTING

2 cups sugar	½ cup water
Pinch of cream of tartar	

When cooked beat in whites of 2 eggs; if too hard, add cold water and beat.

MAPLE FROSTING

Add 1 cup of sweet cream to 3 cups of brown sugar, boil slowly until it will thread from a spoon. This will take about

¾ hour. Then let it get about half cool, stir in 6 drops of Watkins Maple Flavor and ½ cup of chopped nuts, beat until creamy and spread over cake.

UNCOOKED COCOA ICING

Beat white of egg stiff, add powdered sugar until stiff; add little cream and Watkins Vanilla, and 1 heaping teaspoon Watkins Cocoa, and more sugar if necessary. When of right consistency spread on cake.

COCOA ICING

Two cups of sugar mixed with 2 tablespoons of Watkins Cocoa. 1 cup cream. Let boil slowly until it forms a soft ball in water, Stir until thick and creamy and flavor with Watkins Vanilla.

FILLING FOR NUT CAKE

1 pint milk	Salt
1 egg	½ cup sugar
3 tablespoons cornstarch	½ cup chopped nuts

Cook above ingredients with exception of egg, until of a thick creamy consistency. When about half cool add nuts and 1 teaspoon Watkins Vanilla. Use between layers, and use white icing on the top.

RAISIN FILLING

1 cup chopped raisins ½ cup water
1 cup sugar

Boil together until it threads; take off and pour on white of 1 egg; beat until it thickens.

BUTTER FROSTING

⅛ cup butter	2 tablespoons cream
1 cup powdered sugar	1 teaspoon Watkins Vanilla
	or other flavoring

Cream the butter, gradually add sifted sugar and beat until smooth. Add flavoring and cream until of right consistency to spread. Do not spread on a hot cake.

PIES AND PASTRY

A GOOD FOUNDATION FOR PIES

1 heaping cup flour	½ teaspoon salt
Saltspoon of Watkins Bak-	⅓ to ½ cup shortening
ing Powder	Very cold water to mix

Add the salt and baking powder to flour and combine well. Then add about ⅔ of the whole amount of shortening and work it in with the fingertips until the whole is crumbly and like coarse meal. With a knife cut in enough very cold water to make the mixture the right consistency to roll. It should be quite stiff. Reserve ⅓ of the dough for the bottom crust and lay the remainder on a well-floured board, marble or enameled top table, and pat or lightly roll until half an inch in thickness. Put on about ⅓ of the remaining shortening in small amounts, sift a bit of flour over and roll up lightly. Roll out again, proceed as before. The crust is now ready for the pan. When placing crust in pan, press edges down firmly. This amount will make one pie. Grated cheese or ground nuts may be added to the above in small quantities, to give the crust a new and different flavor occasionally.

SNOWDRIFT CHERRY PIE

Line a pie tin with rich pie dough. Fill the crust with canned cherries, using the juice also. Add enough sugar to sweeten and 1 tablespoon flour, working the sugar and flour through the cherries. Place in the oven and bake quickly. When the pie is cool, whip 1 cup of cream until very stiff, sweeten to taste and pile on top of the pie.

ONE-CRUST RAISIN PIE

1 cup of raisins	Pinch of salt
⅔ cup sugar	3 tablespoons cornstarch
½ cup water	2 eggs separated
	½ cup cream

Put sugar, raisins and water on stove to boil. Then mix cream, salt, cornstarch and yolks of eggs together and add to boiling mixture. Cook until thick, pour into a baked pie shell, add meringue and brown.

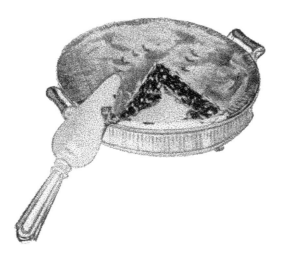

MINCE PIE

When making pies, line deep plate with crust, fill with mince meat, put over top 1 tablespoon cream, 1 tablespoon sugar and bits of butter. Put on top crust and bake 30 minutes in moderate oven. Serve with cubes of Swiss cheese.

MINCEMEAT FOR PIES

2 cups finely chopped lean beef	2 cups sugar
4 cups finely chopped tart apples	1 cup apple cider
2 cups chopped seeded raisins	1 tablespoon Watkins Cloves
2 cups currants	1 tablespoon Watkins Cinnamon
1 cup finely chopped citron	
2 teaspoons salt	1 tablespoon Watkins Nutmeg
1 cup suet chopped or butter	1 cup meat stock
1 cup nuts	

Cook beef and let cool in liquor; then chop. Mix other ingredients in order named. Simmer slowly for 1 hour; bottle and seal hot. This makes about 5 pints.

COCOA PIE

½ cup Watkins Cocoa   3 eggs
1½ cups sugar   2 cups milk
¼ cup cornstarch   2 teaspoons Watkins Vanilla
¾ teaspoon salt

Mix and sift cocoa, sugar, cornstarch and salt. Add unbeaten egg yolks with milk and stir well. Cook in double boiler until thick, stirring constantly. Remove from fire, add vanilla and pour into baked pie crust. Cover with meringue made by beating egg whites until stiff, adding ½ teaspoon Watkins Baking Powder and 6 tablespoons sugar. Brown in oven.

PUMPKIN PIE (EXTRA GOOD)

1 cup of steamed and strained   1 teaspoon Watkins Cinnamon
    pumpkin   3 well beaten eggs
⅔ cup brown sugar   2 cups of cream or rich milk
½ teaspoon Watkins Ginger   ½ teaspoon salt

Mix well. Pour into a pastry lined tin, sprinkle a little sugar over top to make it brown nicely and bake until solid.

PRUNE PIE

Cook prunes until tender and run them through a food chopper. For each pie wanted, add 1 large apple chopped very fine, 1 teaspoon Watkins Cinnamon, 1 teaspoon Watkins Nutmeg, 1 teaspoon Watkins Allspice. Sweeten to taste and dot liberally with butter. Add enough prune juice to make the consistency of mincemeat. Bake in 2 crusts.

Page Forty-Five

LEMON CUSTARD PIE

1 cup sugar	2 tablespoons flour
2 tablespoons butter	1 cup milk
2 eggs	1 lemon, juice and rind

Cream butter and sugar, add well beaten egg yolks and flour and beat well. Then add milk and lemon juice and grated rind. Lastly fold in the well beaten whites. Turn into pie crust and sprinkle Watkins Cinnamon over top. Bake like custard pie.

PINEAPPLE SPONGE PIE

2 cups grated pineapple	⅓ teaspoon Watkins
2 eggs	Lemon Extract
2 tablespoons melted butter	1 tablespoon cornstarch
	1 cup sugar

Beat the egg yolks and sugar together with the cornstarch, add to pineapple with the lemon extract and melted butter. Cut and fold in stiffly beaten egg whites. Pour into plate lined with uncooked pastry and bake until set, or about 20 minutes.

PUDDINGS AND DESSERTS

APPLE SPONGE PUDDING

3 eggs separated	1 teaspoon Watkins Vanilla
1 cup sugar	or Lemon Extract
1 cup flour	1 teaspoon Watkins Baking
½ cup water (scant)	Powder

Beat well, folding in egg whites last.

6 medium sized apples	2 tablespoons butter
	1 pound brown sugar

Pare and divide the apples into eighths. Put in baking dish 2 tablespoons butter. Pour over butter the brown sugar, then the apples and pour batter over all. Bake ¾ to 1 hour in moderate oven. Serve with jellied side on top, with or without cream.

COTTAGE PUDDING

½ cup butter
1 cup sugar
½ cup milk
Pinch of salt

2 eggs
1 large cup flour
1 large teaspoon Watkins
Baking Powder

Beat butter and sugar until creamy; add yolks of eggs, milk, flour, whites of eggs beaten stiff, and 1 teaspoon Watkins Vanilla. Bake ¾ hour in moderate oven in gem tins. Serve with hard sauce, whipped cream or hot chocolate sauce. Or split each cake open, insert 1 tablespoon of strawberry or other preserves, and top with whipped cream.

JELLY CUSTARD WHIP

Make a soft custard, using 2 cups of rich milk, 4 tablespoons of sugar, 1 whole egg beaten, and the beaten yolks of 2. A small amount of finely chopped nuts may be stirred into it when cooked. Pour into 6 sherbet glasses and let cool. Put a small glass of any kind of fruit jelly (strawberry or grape) into a large bowl and beat with Dover egg beater. Add the stiffly beaten whites of 2 eggs. Then beat the whole until stiff. Pile this on the custard in the glasses. A few bits of jelly may be saved for a garnish.

COFFEE JELLY

2 cups clear, strong coffee
1 cup sugar

1½ cups cold water
½ box gelatine

1 cup boiling water

Soak gelatine 3 minutes in cold water; stir in sugar, pour over it boiling water and coffee; strain, and set away to harden. Serve with whipped cream.

COCOA SOUFFLE

Melt 2 tablespoons butter, add 2 tablespoons flour and ¾ cup milk. Add 3 tablespoons cocoa mixed with ⅓ cup sugar and 2 tablespoons hot water. When smooth, add 3 beaten yolks of eggs and cool. Fold in whites of eggs beaten stiff, and ½ teaspoon Watkins Vanilla. Turn into buttered baking dish and bake 25 minutes in moderate oven.

STEAMED CHOCOLATE PUDDING

2 tablespoons Watkins Cocoa   2 eggs
2½ tablespoons butter   ½ cup milk
½ cup sugar   2 scant cups flour
1 teaspoon Watkins Vanilla   2 scant teaspoons Watkins
     Baking Powder

Cream butter and sugar, add eggs one at a time, and beat well. Add cocoa mixed with flour and baking powder and ½ cup milk alternately. Lastly add melted butter. Put in mold and steam 3 hours. Serve with hard sauce.

ARME RITTER

Sift together 1½ cups of flour, 2 teaspoons of Watkins Baking Powder, ¼ teaspoon salt and 2 tablespoons powdered sugar. Beat 1 egg, add ⅔ cup milk and to this add the dry ingredients. Stir to a smooth batter, which should be thin enough to coat whatever is dropped into it. Prepare 8 or 10 slices of rather stale bread, cut quite thin. Spread half of them with jam and butter the others, spreading the butter quite thin. Press together in sandwich fashion the buttered slices over those spread with jam. Cut in strips or fancy shapes. Dip in batter and fry in deep fat. Drain, sprinkle with sugar and serve with lemon sauce.

WATKINS COCOA SYRUP

(For Ice Cream, Puddings, etc.)

1 cup Watkins Cocoa   2 cups sugar
Dash of salt   2 cups boiling water
     2 teaspoons Watkins Vanilla

Mix and sift cocoa, sugar and salt. Add boiling water and stir well. Boil 25 minutes. Remove from fire and add vanilla. Cool and place in sterilized jars; seal and keep in refrigerator until ready for use.

FROZEN COCOA PUDDING

1 quart milk	½ teaspoon salt
1½ cups sugar	2 tablespoons cornstarch

½ cup Watkins Cocoa

Put the milk on to heat in a double boiler; mix the cornstarch, cocoa, sugar and salt with a little of the cold milk until smooth; then add them to the hot milk and cook for 15 minutes. When cold put in the freezer and freeze. If necessary canned milk may be used instead of fresh milk.

COCOA MARSHMALLOW ROLL

Mix ½ cup sugar with 2 tablespoons Watkins Cocoa. Then add 2 eggs and beat until very light. Stir in 1 tablespoon of melted butter, then ½ cup of pastry flour sifted with ¾ teaspoon of Watkins Baking Powder. Pour into a greased shallow pan and bake in a moderate oven for 12 to 15 minutes. Turn out on a piece of brown paper sprinkled with powdered sugar. Spread with marshmallow whip or cream and roll up like a jelly roll. Wrap the paper or a cloth around it and let stand until cold. Ice with chocolate frosting.

SALADS

WALNUT SALAD

Mix equal quantities of cut celery, apples and chopped walnuts and serve on lettuce leaf with following dressing:

1 tablespoon sweet cream	1 tablespoon sugar

2 tablespoons Watkins Prepared Mustard

BUTTERFLY SALAD

Cut a slice of pineapple in halves and place on lettuce leaf with rounded edges together. This represents wings of the butterfly. Slice a very small banana into quarters lengthwise and place one strip between the rounded edges of the pineapple to form the body. For eyes put in tiny bits of raisins. Cut fine strips of pimentos for feelers or use pieces of maraschino cherries. Serve with cooked salad dressing, which is placed on the lettuce leaf beside the butterfly.

EGG AND POTATO SALAD

5 cold potatoes   6 or 8 hard boiled eggs

Slice eggs and potatoes.

DRESSING

1 cup sweet or sour cream   1 teaspoon salt
3 tablespoons vinegar   ½ teaspoon Watkins ground
                                  Mustard

Steam this in double boiler. When it has come to a boil add 1
egg beaten light and stir constantly. Remove from fire shortly
after egg has been added. Pour over sliced eggs and potatoes and
mix well. Garnish with parsley or lettuce and serve.

ORANGE CUP SALAD

½ cup dates   3 oranges
½ cup figs   ¾ cup sugar
                .   ½ cup pineapple

Halve the oranges; remove pulp; put shells on ice to stiffen. Cut
the fruit into small pieces, add a little sugar and mix together
thoroughly with a dressing made from Watkins Prepared Mustard.
(See dressing recipe under Walnut Salad.) Fill each shell with the
mixture and put whipped cream on top. Serve on lettuce leaves.

FRUIT SALAD

24 marshmallows   2 juicy apples
1 can pineapple   6 oranges
½ cup nut meats

Cut fruit and marshmallows into small pieces, then mix and chill.

DRESSING

1 tablespoon butter   2 tablespoons vinegar
Pinch of salt   2 eggs
2 tablespoons sugar   ½ pint whipped cream
1 teaspoon Watkins ground Mustard

Beat up eggs in double boiler, add vinegar, sugar, salt, butter and mustard and cook until thick. Cool and add whipped cream. Pour off surplus juice from chilled fruit, add nuts and mix dressing with fruit and serve on lettuce.

TOMATO JELLY SALAD

½ can or 2 cups tomatoes   1 teaspoon salt
1 slice onion   2 teaspoons sugar
3 whole cloves   ½ teaspoon Watkins Pepper
1 bay leaf   2 tablespoons gelatine soaked
in ½ cup cold water

Boil tomatoes with onion and seasoning until soft. Strain and add soaked gelatine, stirring until dissolved. Pour into molds. Serve on beds of shredded celery and lettuce with mayonnaise.

STUFFED APPLE SALAD

Pare and core firm apples. Simmer gently in water to which tiny red cinnamon candies have been added. These serve for sweetening and give color and flavor. Cool. Place on lettuce leaf, fill centers with cottage cheese and nuts or chopped raisins and nuts, add salad dressing and serve.

CANDLESTICK SALAD

Place a whole slice of pineapple on a salad plate. Cut a straight banana in halves crosswise. Stand half of the banana in upright position in center of pineapple slice. Make a cut in tip of banana and insert a third of a red maraschino cherry for a flame. Serve with mayonnaise or boiled dressing placed at one side of the pineapple.

SHRIMP SALAD

2 tablespoons butter	1 lemon
1 can shrimps	4 tablespoons vinegar
1 cup celery cut fine	2 tablespoons water
1 cup tart apple cubes	4 eggs
1 cup nuts	1 teaspoon Watkins ground
Salt and pepper to taste	Mustard
1 cup whipped cream	1 teaspoon salt
½ cup thick cream	1 teaspoon sugar

Break shrimps into pieces in bowl, moisten with a little melted butter, season with vinegar, salt and pepper. Put apple cubes in small dish and sprinkle lightly with lemon juice, then put in celery with a little more lemon juice and toss together. Cover and set aside. Heat vinegar and water in double boiler, beat eggs, and gradually add to vinegar, stirring constantly. Add butter and cook slowly, still stirring. Remove from fire and beat till cold, then add mustard, salt, sugar and pepper. Add thick cream just before serving. When ready to serve toss nuts, celery, apple and shrimps together and a little dressing. Heap on crisp lettuce leaves on individual plates and pour over each salad a heaping spoon of dressing and top with spoon of unsweetened whipped cream.

SALAD DRESSINGS

FRUIT SALAD DRESSING

Beat juice of 2 oranges, 3 lemons and 2 eggs; add ½ cup sugar and boil in double boiler until clear. Whip 1 cup cream and stir thoroughly into mixture; set away to cool.

COMBINATION DRESSING

½ cup olive oil	Little chopped parsley
2½ tablespoons vinegar	⅛ tablespoon chopped pimento
¼ small onion minced	½ tablespoon green pepper
1 teaspoon Watkins Prepared Mustard	¼ teaspoon salt
	Pinch of powdered sugar

Add 1 ingredient at a time, mixing thoroughly with spoon. Let stand ½ hour and use on any green salad.

RUSSIAN DRESSING

4 tablespoons tomato catsup	1 teaspoon chopped green and red peppers
1 hard boiled egg chopped fine	2 tablespoons olive oil
½ tablespoon vinegar	1 tablespoon Watkins Prepared Mustard
Dash of Watkins Red Pepper	

Mix oil, vinegar, catsup and Watkins Prepared Mustard thoroughly. Then stir in lightly the remaining ingredients, leaving the chopped egg until the last.

MAYONNAISE DRESSING

1 egg yolk	Dash of Watkins Red Pepper
½ teaspoon Watkins ground Mustard	1 cup salad oil
½ teaspoon salt	2 tablespoons vinegar or lemon juice

Utensils and ingredients should be very cold. Put egg yolk in shallow bowl, add seasoning and mix well. Add oil slowly, almost drop by drop, beating until thick. Thin with vinegar and continue adding oil and vinegar until all is used. Juice of lemon may be substituted for vinegar.

Page Fifty-Three

HONEY SALAD DRESSING FOR FRUIT SALAD

3 egg yolks
½ cup strained honey
1 tablespoon sugar

⅓ cup lemon juice
Grated rind of lemon
½ cup sweet whipped cream

Beat eggs until frothy; add honey, sugar, lemon juice and rind. Put on fire in double boiler and cook, stirring constantly until as thick as heavy cream. When cool add ½ cup whipped cream.

FRENCH DRESSING

Mix in dish ½ teaspoon salt, a bit of Watkins ground Mustard, sugar, a bit of Watkins Black Pepper and Red Pepper and 4 tablespoons olive oil; add 1 tablespoon vinegar. Ingredients should be very cold. Beat until thick and serve on vegetable and meat salads.

JELLIES AND PRESERVES

GRAPE JELLY

Select grapes not fully ripe; wash, drain; put in kettle and mash well; heat until all skins are broken and juice flows freely; strain and put through a flannel bag. Measure; bring to boiling point and boil 5 minutes. Add heated sugar (pint to pint) to juice and boil 3 minutes; skim; pour in glasses. Place in sun; let stand 24 hours and cover with paraffine.

APPLE MINT JELLY

Cut up white tart apples. Cover with boiling water, cover and let cook undisturbed until soft. Turn into pan. For every quart of apple juice, heat 3 cups of sugar in a pan in the oven. Set juice over fire with 1 bunch of mint leaves in a cheesecloth bag. Cook 20 minutes; strain into clean saucepan. Heat to boiling point; add hot sugar, let boil until it jellies slightly when tested. Tint with green vegetable coloring, either liquid or paste. Have jelly glasses filled with water, turn out and pour in jelly. This is very good to serve with meats.

PINEAPPLE AND GOOSEBERRY RELISH

2 cups gooseberries   3 cups sugar
1 cup pineapple

Put pineapple through grinder, mix with gooseberries and sugar and cook until thick like jam. Put in glasses as for jelly.

GRAPE CONSERVE

One basket grapes. Cook without water and mash through colander. Add peels of 3 oranges, which have been cooked separately 10 minutes previously, 6 cups sugar, 1 package seedless raisins, and the juice of 5 oranges. 1 cup of walnuts when almost done. Cook 25 minutes.

PEACH CONSERVE

Very ripe peaches and as much sugar, ½ pound walnuts to 1 quart peaches, 1 orange and 1 grated rind; simmer slowly.

SPICED CURRANTS

7 pounds currants   2 tablespoons Watkins Cinnamon
5 pounds brown sugar   2 tablespoons Watkins Cloves
1 pint vinegar   1 teaspoon Watkins Allspice

Pick over the currants, wash, drain and remove the stems. Put in a kettle, add the sugar, vinegar and the spices. Bring to a boil and let simmer until it is of the consistency of heavy marmalade or jam, which will be about 1 hour. Store in a stone jar and keep in a cool place.

ORANGE MARMALADE

Use only the pulp from 2 grapefruit. Slice 6 oranges and 4 lemons thin and cut in small pieces; place in preserving kettle over night with 3 quarts of water; add 3 pounds of cane sugar. In the morning boil until it is like jelly. Three pounds of sugar is a little over 2 quarts.

CANNED STRAWBERRIES

Wash and hull berries. Use 4 pounds sugar to 6 pounds of berries and 6 cups of water; let berries stand with sugar over night; in the morning add water and let boil up quickly; skim and can.

PICKLES AND RELISHES

MUSTARD PICKLES

2 quarts small pickles	2 heads celery
2 quarts white onions	2 cups sugar
2 quarts green beans	$\frac{3}{4}$ cup flour
2 heads cauliflower	$\frac{1}{2}$ cup Watkins ground Mustard
3 green peppers	1 egg
3 red peppers	1 ounce butter
2 grated carrots	$2\frac{1}{2}$ quarts vinegar

$1\frac{1}{2}$ teaspoons turmeric powder

Let cucumbers stand in salt and a little alum and water 24 hours. Boil onions in salt and water, not too tender. Cook beans in salt and water. Cook cauliflower in lots of water. Slice peppers and cut celery fine. Cook sugar, flour, mustard, egg, butter, vinegar and turmeric powder as for salad dressing. Boil celery, onions and carrots in dressing. Combine all vegetables with dressing mixture and seal hot.

SLICED CUCUMBER PICKLES

Slice large cucumbers and cover with salt water over night. Fill 2 quart jars with cucumbers. Add 2 teaspoons Watkins Mustard, 2 teaspoons sugar, 1 teaspoon Watkins Mixed Spices and 1 teaspoon celery seed. Fill jar with cold vinegar and seal.

DILL PICKLES

50 medium cucumbers	$1\frac{1}{2}$ cups salt
1 large bunch dill	6 quarts water
$\frac{1}{2}$ cup mustard seed	$\frac{1}{2}$ cup grated horse-radish

$1\frac{1}{2}$ quarts vinegar

Place cucumbers to soak over night by using 1 cup of salt to each gallon of water. In the morning drain and arrange them in layers in glass fruit jars. Place on top of each layer some of the dill, horse-radish and mustard seed. Heat together the vinegar, water and salt and pour it boiling hot over cucumbers and seal.

CORN RELISH

1 quart vinegar	
3 tablespoons Watkins ground Mustard	} Boil together
20 ears of corn	2 red peppers
4 large onions	2 cups sugar
1 head cabbage	½ cup salt
2 green peppers	2 teaspoons celery seed

Boil all together about ½ hour; watch closely that it does not burn. Seal hot.

CRAB APPLE PICKLES

Crab apples	1 pound sugar
1 cup vinegar	1 ounce Watkins Cloves
1 ounce Watkins Allspice	2 ounces Watkins Cinnamon

Use the whole spices, taking them from a package of Watkins Mixed Spices, and put them in a little cheesecloth bag; drop the bag into the vinegar and boil 5 or 8 minutes; clean the apples, remove the blossom end and cook in the hot vinegar until tender; seal in jars. Remove spice bag from vinegar so apples will not be discolored.

CANDIES AND CONFECTIONS

CHRISTMAS PUDDING CANDY

3 cups sugar	1 pound dates
1 cup light cream	1 pound figs
1 heaping tablespoon butter	1 pound raisins
1 teaspoon Watkins Vanilla	1 pound cocoanut
1 or 2 cups nuts	

Cook sugar, cream and butter to soft ball. Beat until creamy, then beat in fruit and nuts. If cocoanut is coarse, grind it. When well mixed, roll as for meat loaf. Wrap in dampened cloth, then in waxed paper and put away to ripen. Make at least 2 weeks before you wish to use it. When wanted, slice in squares and oblongs.

COCOA FUDGE

1 cup Watkins Cocoa	3 tablespoons butter
4 cups white sugar	1 teaspoon Watkins Vanilla
2 cups milk	1 cup chopped nuts

Sift cocoa and sugar together; add milk and stir well. Place over fire, bring to boiling point and boil gently until a little dropped in cold water forms a soft ball. Do not stir during the boiling process. Remove from fire, add butter and let cool. Then add vanilla and chopped nuts and beat until creamy. Pour into buttered pan and mark into squares before it hardens.

CREAM NUT LOAF

6 cups white sugar	1 pound English walnuts
1 cup white syrup	3 cups light cream
1 tablespoon butter	1½ teaspoons Watkins Vanilla

Boil sugar, syrup and cream until it forms a soft ball when tested in cold water. Remove from fire, add butter and beat until it thickens. Add nuts and vanilla and when nearly ready to set, pour into buttered loaf tin to cool. Slice and cut in squares.

MAPLE FUDGE

3 cups brown sugar	1 teaspoon Watkins Maple
1 cup cream	Flavor
1 cup nuts	

Boil sugar and cream until it forms soft ball in cold water. Beat until light, add nuts and flavoring and turn into buttered dish. Mark in squares.

SALTED NUTS

Cover nuts with boiling water; let stand 2 minutes; drain; put in cold water and rub off skins. Place on tins and put in oven and dry—don't let brown. Take from oven and add 1 tablespoon melted butter to ½ pound of nuts. Put back in oven and brown; Take out and salt.

BEVERAGES

GRAPE HI-BALL LEMONADE

Juice of 3 lemons
1½ pints of water
1 cup sugar
1 tablespoon Watkins Grape Hi-Ball

Mix lemon juice with other ingredients. Turn into pitcher half filled with ice and stir thoroughly. Let stand 10 minutes before serving.

MINT RASPBERRY PUNCH

¼ cup orange juice
½ cup lemon juice
½ cup sugar
1 pint cold water
1 tablespoon Watkins Raspberry
½ doz. sprigs of fresh mint

Mix fruit juices, sugar and Watkins Raspberry; stir well and add water. Pour over large pieces of ice. Serve with a sprig of mint in each glass.

GRAPE PUNCH

Juice of 2 oranges
Juice of 2 lemons
2 tablespoons Watkins Grape Hi-Ball
1 cup sugar
6 tumblers water

Mix ingredients well and chill with ice. This provides individual service for eight.

CHILLED CHERRY TEA

Prepare your favorite tea in quantity required. Chill with ice. Add 2 teaspoons Watkins Cherry Cluster to each glass served. Stir well. Sweeten as desired.

ICED COCOA

3 tablespoons Watkins Cocoa
½ cup sugar
1 cup boiling water

Mix and add 1 quart scalded milk. Stir well; chill and serve with a spoonful of whipped cream. Quantity 5 or 6 glasses.

ICED COCOA FOR THIRTY

3 cups boiling water
¾ cup Watkins Cocoa
2½ cups sugar

Stir until well dissolved. Place in double boiler and cook 30 minutes. Cool and add 1 tablespoon Watkins Vanilla Flavor and 6 quarts of scalded milk. Chill, beat well. Serve in chilled glasses. Place a spoonful cracked ice in each glass, add cocoa, and top with whipped cream.

MOCHA NECTAR

1 cup strong coffee (Watkins)   3 cups Watkins Cocoa pre-
Serve with chipped ice   pared with milk

HOT COCOA

Take one teaspoonful each of Watkins Cocoa and sugar for every cup. Mix thoroughly, add boiling water to make a paste. Add required amount of hot milk, or milk and water mixed, to produce desired richness. Boil about five minutes. Sweeten and serve. Add a marshmallow to each cup, if preferred, or top with whipped cream.

KITCHEN WEIGHTS AND MEASURES

60 drops.........................1 teaspoon
3 teaspoons......................1 tablespoon
16 tablespoons wet..................1 cup
16 tablespoons dry..................1 cup
1 cup............................½ pint or 2 gills
2 cups...........................1 pint
2 pints..........................1 quart
4 quarts.........................1 gallon
8 quarts.........................1 peck dry
1 heaping tablespoon sugar..........1 ounce
1 heaping tablespoon butter or
     butter size of an egg............2 ounces or ¼ cup
2 heaping tablespoons cocoa.........1 square chocolate
Juice of one lemon.................3 tablespoons
1 cup butter......................½ pound
2 cups granulated sugar.............1 pound
2½ cups powdered sugar.............1 pound
2⅓ cups brown sugar...............1 pound
4 cups flour......................1 pound
2 cups rice.......................1 pound
2 cups chopped meat...............1 pound
2 cups chopped suet...............1 pound
3 cups raisins....................1 pound
4⅓ cups coffee....................1 pound
1 cup chopped nut meats............¼ pound

When sour milk is used 1 even teaspoon soda to a pint of milk.

1 teaspoon of baking powder is the equivalent of ½ teaspoon of soda and 1 teaspoon of cream of tartar.

INDEX TO RECIPES

WATKINS COOK BOOK

INDEX TO RECIPES—Continued

Watkins Products

QUALITY :: ECONOMY :: CONVENIENCE

FOOD PRODUCTS

Baking Powder
Cocoa
Prepared Mustard
Red Color
Coffee
Candy Mints—Four Flavors
Chewing Gum—Two Flavors

Extracts and Flavors—
 Almond, Banana
 Cinnamon, Lemon
 Maple, Mixed Fruit
 Orange, Pineapple
 Strawberry
 Vanilla Straight
 Vanillin and Coumarin
 Vanilla, Vanillin and Coumarin

Spices—
 Allspice   Cinnamon
 Cloves   Ginger
 Mustard   Nutmeg
 Pepper   Sage
 Red Pepper
 Mixed Pickling Spices

Fruit Flavors—
 Imitation Cherry
 Imitation Grape
 Imitation Raspberry

MEDICINES

After Dinner Tablets
Aspirin
Blood and Skin Alterative Tonic
Cascara-Senna Compound Tablets
Catarrh Medicine
Cathartic Liver Pills
Chill Tonic
Compound Mustard Ointment
Corn Salve
Cough Balsam
Cough Medicine
Cream of Camphor
Digestive Tablets
Diuretic Tablets
Female Tonic
Gen-De-Can-Dra
Headache Tablets
Herb Tablets
Kidney and Bladder Pills

Laxative Cold and Grip Tablets
Laxative Syrup, Lax-Tone
Laxative Wafers
Liniment
Little Liver Pills
Menthol-Camphor Ointment
Mouth Wash and Liquid Antiseptic
Pain Oil, Pain-Oleum
Petro-Carbo Salve
Rheumatic and Gout Pills
Root and Herb Tea
Sarsaparilla
Skin Ointment
Toothache Wax
Volatyle Salve
Worm Tablets

TOILET ARTICLES

Brown Skin Face Powder
Cocoanut Oil Shampoo
Cold Cream
Complexion Powder
Cosmetic Lotion
Dandruff Remover and Scalp Tonic
Deodorant Powder
Face Cream
Fragrant Pomade

Perfumes—
 Bouquet, Jockey Club
 Lily of the Valley
 Trefle, Rose, Violet

Shampoo Jelly
Shaving Cream
Talcum Powder—
 Egyptian Bouquet
 Perfumed, Violet

Toilet Water—
 Lilac Lily Rose Violet

Tooth Brushes, two sizes
Tooth Paste, Tooth Powder
Vanishing Cream
Wistaria Cream

Belle de Nuit Line—
 Cream
  Cleansing, Vanishing
  Emollient
 Face Powder
  Pink, Medium, Natural
 Perfume
  Large and purse sizes

Belle de Nuit Line—Continued
 Talcum Powder
 Toilet Water
 Compact
  Single, Double, Refills
 Gift Boxes

Garda Line—
 Cream
 Face Powder
  Brunette, Flesh
  Natural, White
 Nail Polish
 Perfume
 Rouge
  Dark, Medium, Peche
 Talcum Powder
 Toilet Water

SOAPS AND CLEANSERS

Washing Compound
Shredsope
WAT Soap Flakes
Baby
Cold Cream
Crystal Rose
Germicidal
Green Palm
Mineral Bath
Refined Pine Tar
Shaving
Skin Soap, medicated
Vegetable Oil
Witch Hazel

STOCK AND POULTRY PREPARATIONS

Fly Oil   Louse Killer
Stock Dip   Stock Tonic
Poultry Tonic
Antiseptic Healing Powder
Veterinary Ointment

MISCELLANEOUS

Hy Powder
Furniture and Auto Polish
Household Disinfectant
Pencils
Sewing Machine Oil

PRINTED IN U. S. A.

ND - #0039 - 291222 - C0 - 229/152/4 [6] - CB - 9780331179651 - Gloss Lamination